DEDICATION

This book is dedicated to you the reader. You are the one who is struggling with this disease that has rocked your world to the core. You are the one who had to sort and sift through this foreign language and figure out what all of these words and treatment options mean. Maybe up until that day when your doctor said, "you have cancer," you thought all chemotherapy was the same. Now you know that chemotherapy comes patient and cancer specific. It is not a one size fits all treatment. You have wrestled through all of that to make the best decisions that you could with the information you had.

You deserve this book dedicated to you. You are the one going to the medical appointments , treatments, losing your hair, energy, and fighting to hold on to joy, peace and happiness. You are doing the best you can and you deserve to applaud yourself and do a little happy dance. This book is all about you. It is written with you in mind.

This book is intended to be simple, easy and practical, using twenty -six words, the ABC's of the alphabet They were carefully chosen and tooled to help you focus on one thing you can put in action or just think about on a daily basis to help you cope with the stress and distress of this process. Some words will distract you from your day in and day out process and some words like, REGRET will take you deep within yourself. The words are playful and serious. Remember, these words were chosen just for you. Cherish yourself and move gently through this journey. It is a journey, it is not a destination. Enjoy and cherish each moment you have. None of us are guaranteed the next moment. Make this moment yours. Keep up the good work. You are worth it.

BOOKS

Breast Cancer: A-Z Mindful Practices
Self Care Tools for Treatment & Recovery
Dr. Robin B Dilley

Writing Your Way To Healing and Wholeness
Dr. Robin B Dilley

In A Moment's Notice, A Psychiatrist's Journey With
Breast Cancer
Dr. Robin B. Dilley

WEBSITES

PSYCHOTHERAPYUNLIMITED.COM

BREASTCANCERYOGABLOG.COM

A B C

WORKBOOK

for

CANCER
PATIENTS

Let's heal one letter at a time.

DR. ROBIN B. DILLEY

ACKNOWLEDGEMENT

The Cover Design was completed by Desiree Lange. You see the maze in the background. The maze is a complex system of decisions, choices, and changes. A cancer diagnosis is like a maze. You start out on one path and very soon find yourself at choice points where you must decide which direction to take or even back-track. Mazes are difficult to navigate and often you may experience being lost. The goal is to keep putting one foot in front of the other and do the best you can at the time.

As you delve into this book you will find the L word is about the Labyrinth. The labyrinth is an ancient symbol found throughout the world. The Labyrinth is a unicursal path, one way to the center and the same way back out again. Walking a labyrinth provides you an opportunity to tap into your deepest wisdom in the center and receive what you need at this moment. When you are feeling lost in this medical maze allow yourself to take a walk on a labyrinth, releasing your anxiety and finding your center of peace for the moment. This medical maze is a process and you will find yourself frustrated and afraid at times. Keep walking. Don't give up. There are tools in this book that will help you keep on your path and negotiate the decisions that you will have to make.

ABC Workbook For Cancer Patients
Let's Heal One Letter At A Time

First Published in 2018
Published By Psychotherapy Unlimited
PsychotherapyUnlimited.com

Library of Congress Cataloging-in-Publication Data
ABC Workbook For Cancer Patients: Let's Heal One Letter At A Time /
Dr. Robin B. Dilley, 1st edition
Dawn Bradford Editor

ISBN-10: 1721678026
ISBN-13: 978-1721678020
1. Psychology 2. Cancer 3. Alternative Treatments I. ABC Workbook For
Cancer Patients

This publication contains the opinion and ideas of its author. It is intended to provide helpful and informative materials on the subjects addressed in the publication. It is sold with the understanding that the author and publisher are not engaged in rendering medical, health, or any other kind of personal professional services in the book. The reader should consult with his or her medical, health or other competent professional before adopting any of the suggestions in this book or drawing inferences from it.

PSYCHOTHERAPY UNLIMITED

To order visit
Author's website at Psychotherapy Unlimited
(602)564-1919 Phoenix, Arizona 85083
Publisher's website at Breast Cancer Yoga

A B C

WORKBOOK

for

CANCER
PATIENTS

Let's heal one letter at a time.

DR. ROBIN B. DILLEY

TABLE OF CONTENTS

INTRODUCTION

INTRODUCTION
WHY
THE TOOL-BOX?

I invite you to think of this book as pages filled with words that will become your tool-box.

I think it is important to stay away from words that create images of good and bad. I think words like war and warrior are often misconstrued as us against them. However, I wanted to write a book about cancer that men could relate to as well as women. I wanted to create a book for people.

I believe men are underserved in this world of cancer. Men will not normally sit around and talk about their prostate cancer as women do about breast cancer. Men will not usually share their feelings about cancers such as lung, brain, or even talk about their heart disease. Thus, it is my belief when men are perusing book titles on cancer,

3

that even the word "warrior" may seem exhausting to them. Societal norms have forced men to be strong, fight, and get over it. As a result, of those strong socialized norms, the mortality rate for men with cancer is higher than women with cancer. I believe this is because men often put off doctor's appointments, self-care, and treatment. They don't talk about their symptoms until it is too late. Early detection for all cancers is the key to the best possible outcome. Cancer makes people feel vulnerable and vulnerability is hard to tolerate. Avoidance can set in and keep you from getting the medical attention you need. Then there is shame. The S word in this book is shame. You can sneak ahead to see what I am going to say about it. This is not a book you have to read in order. You can pick it up and read any word that speaks to you on any given day. This book is not linear nor chronological. And this book is not just a book for men. It is a book for everyone. All people have used tools in his/her life to make it a more palatable place to be. Thus, the word Tool-Box was born.

Tool boxes come in all shapes and sizes based on people's needs. Some of you are quite happy to have a very portable and efficient tool-box which usually includes a tape-measure, a hammer, a screw-driver, maybe a Philips screw-driver too, and a pair of pliers. With these essential tools, you can fix almost anything, create new things, and get into tough places.

Others are mortified at the thought of your tools fitting into a small compact portable box. Those of you need all the tools that you can possibly imagine for any problem that might come up. For instance, you would need a drill, a saw, an entire wrench set, multiple screw-drivers, a level, and the list goes on. Then some of you are specialist and need a tool box for car maintenance, plumbing, electric and so on. You get the picture.

Coping with Cancer requires a tool-box too. Each of you will decide how big your tool-box will be. Some of you will want the basic and some of your will want the deluxe. Some of you will be comfortable using the typical western medicine available to us in mid-stream America. Your tool-box will contain your family practice doctor, oncologist, radiologist, and surgeon. Some of you will want a tool box of both traditional and integrative medicine. You want all the folks listed above on your team as well as an integrative medicine specialist, homeopathy, massage, yoga and the assistance of a naturopathic doctor and a psychologist. Some of you may be comfortable only going with alternative methods. What is in your tool-box is your personal decision. I personally see the basic tool-box as an essential starting place for treatment with cancer. Then you can add to your tool-box with alternative care options and some holistic assistance.

This book is designed to help you be mindful during this time of treatment. It follows a similar pattern of my book, Breast Cancer: A-Z Mindful Practices. It is designed to help you think, cope, respond, and practice self-help tools that will make this journey a little easier for you along your path. You might even want to think of it as a flashlight in your tool-box. It will help you explore, examine, and expand your awareness of the many ways of coping with this challenging disease.

There are some difficult chapters that may bring up challenging emotions like regrets and forgiveness. The diagnosis of cancer rips away the veil of mortality leaving you facing the possibility of death. That possibility often leads to a life review of wishes, desires, wants, and regrets. All of those will get addressed in very short but deliberate ways.

It is also important to note that this book will speak about spirituality, relationship to God or the divine. I do not suggest any specific religion or spiritual practice, but I do believe cancer gives us an opportunity to figure out just exactly what each of us believes about God, spirit and soul. I believe cancer invites us to explore more deeply and personally, who God is to us and what names we are most comfortable using when speaking of the spiritual world. Thus, many of the words in this book will refer to spiritual selves, spirituality, divine, and God. You will see words like Buddhism, Native American Spirituality, Judaism and others. I believe cancer is better managed with some sort of spiritual component or belief system that helps us make meaning out of our day to day life. For instance, I do not believe God had anything at all to do with my getting cancer, but I found spirituality to be very comforting and strengthening for me as I came to understand and accept the cancer as part of my life's story.

I think the Life of Pi is an amazing story and it gives us plenty of tools and things to think about as we face our cancer. The movie ends with a very reflective question, "Which story do you prefer to believe?" It is the same with cancer. You can choose to be a victim thinking that this awful thing has happened to you or even sent to you by the gods that be, or you can choose to open the tool box of coping materials and figure out on a day to day basis how to better cope with this nasty disease that has entered your body. The choice is yours and somedays it will be easier than others to use the tools and other days you will wrap up in a blanket and go back to bed. Let yourself have some of those days too just don't live there.

May this book become you ally and friend and may the pages in it become well-worn. May you experience hope and moments of blessing on this journey of yours. If you want to contact me, you can go to my web-page at http://www.psychotherapyunlimited.com

ABC WORKBOOK

10

ACTION
LEARN TO
STAY ON TASK

Wow! Here you sit, your world disheveled and upside down. Your mind split in 1000 directions. Is there a hole to climb into? Is this cancer diagnosis a nightmare or a huge mistake? Nope. Here it is in front of you, the pathology report. You keep checking the name making sure it is yours. Now what do you do?

Regardless of what your feelings are right now or the amount of fear that cancer raises up inside of you, you must take ACTION.

ACTION is your friend. ACTION is one of the most important things to do.You will learn some very important things in this and one is how to be the captain of your own treatment team. You will learn to ask questions, lots of questions as part of your ACTION plan.

As you become acquainted with the twenty-six words in this book you will most likely learn to stay on task, stay inspired and take the necessary ACTION to help yourself heal. It is all about healing right now. Cancer is not what it used to be. It is no longer a death sentence and you and the actions you take are the most important part of making it a healing opportunity verses a death sentence.

Your attitude towards this cancer will make a huge difference in how you cope and move through treatment. The ACTIONS you take will help your attitude remain positive. You can do these ACTIONS. Yes, it will be, scary at times, but even when it is scary keep taking positive steps toward healing, then you will remain an active part of your treatment team.

Being passive is not a luxury that you can afford right now. You cannot just sign your life away for your treatment team to make all of the decisions for you. You must be a person of direction, knowledge and filled with hope. You are going to have a whole new language to learn and you are going to have to learn it fast. Even words like "pathology report" are brand new to you. Be sure to ask for a copy of each report you receive. You will want copies of all your pathology reports, blood work, CT scans, MRI reports, etc. Right now, it does not matter if you understand the reports; but you will have your own file to take to new doctors, second opinions, and to compare your progress to in the future.

Let this word ACTION be your guide over the next few months as your life becomes more complex. Your days will be filled with doctor's appointments, treatments, and medical procedures. It will calm down, but not for a while.

ACTION STEPS TO TAKE EVERYDAY
1. **Question and Research.**
2. **Seek a second opinion.**
3. **Explore complimentary medicine.**
4. **Change your life with dietary changes and exercise.**
5. **Read articles on your diagnosis.**
6. **Establish a treatment team you trust.**
7. **Risk saying "No."**
8. **Remember there are no silly questions.**

You are the most important person on this journey. Take care of yourself first and delegate everyone else to second place.

ACTION in big steps and little steps get you closer to how you want to embrace this journey. As you keep putting one foot in front of the other you will come to a place where you feel more confident in your choices and move forward into your healing.

THE HELPFUL PRACTICES:
1. **List 3 actions steps to take in the morning.**
2. **Journal 10 minutes on how you are feeling and coping.**
3. **List 3 gratitudes at night.**

BREATHE
TO CALM &
CONTROL ANXIETY

Maybe it is because I am a psychologist and help my clients engage in the practice of focused breathing, that I can hear your inner chatter shouting out negative messages to me right now. For instance, some are you are saying things like, "I have cancer and you want me to focus on my breathing. Get real." Others of you are saying, "How is learning to BREATHE differently going to help me now?" Those thoughts re completely reasonable reactions, but if you can trust me, conscious breath can invite positive benefits through-out your journey.

For you to modulate your anxiety during these trying days of learning to live with your cancer diagnosis, it is important to use your BREATH in therapeutic ways. You have been breathing all your life from the moment someone slapped your behind at birth; however, conscious breathing can calm your anxiety and lower your blood pressure, which is important during this time.

Try this simple exercise for a few minutes every day and use these methods while you wait for the doctor, or late at night when you are wide awake with worry.

You will find various exercises on BREATHING if you Google breathing exercises. One of my favorites is by Andrew Weil M.D. It is called the 4-7-8 Breathe. Breathe in to the count of 4. Hold for the count of 7. Breath out while counting to 8. Repeat this four times and notice the difference. If you Google it you will find a video of Dr. Weil demonstrating it.

The point is that with all the mindfulness practices available to us today, the most important one of all is your BREATH. Yoga teachers, psychologists, teachers, and medical professionals are all teaching clients to practice focused breathing techniques to help calm down and live more conscious lives.

If you are experiencing lots of fear and major panic with this diagnosis of yours then you may have to practice this BREATH work often throughout the day.

BREATH-WORK

1. **Turn your attention to your body.**
2. **Make your body comfortable where you are sitting or lying.**
3. **Close your eyes.**
4. **BREATHE in through your nostrils slowly.**
5. **Hold your breath for a moment (maybe to the count of four).**
6. **Slowly exhale through your mouth.**
7. **Repeat this process 4-6 times.**

8. **Notice your body again.**
9. **What is different?**

It is not a one-time magic pill, but it is the most helpful friend you will have for the rest of your life if you choose to discipline your mind. These amazing techniques will carry you happily and healthily into your future.

THREE HELPFUL PRACTICES:

1. **Set your timer for three minutes and inhale and exhale slowly for three minutes. Notice what begins to happen to your body.**

2. **At night inhale and exhale ten times and repeat until sleep takes over.**

3. **When you must make a difficult phone call or talk about what is happening with you and your cancer, notice the tears coming to the surface, and take a moment to turn your attention to your BREATH. Inhale and exhale as slow as possible for a few breaths and resume talking again. You might be delighted that you are able to keep those tears at bay until you have finished saying what you need to say.**

BONUS PRACTICE: Buy some old-fashioned bubbles and use the bubbles to help you grieve and BREATHE. This action will automatically teach you how to BREATHE correctly.

COURAGE
HOW TO BUILD A DISCIPLINED MIND

What is courage and how do you get courage now that you need it more than ever?

While choosing to create new COURAGEOUS plans moving forward, just remember to always look back to see where you've been. Remember in the Wizard of Oz that each character already had what they needed without realizing it? Recall how Scarecrow thinks and problem solves; the Tin-Man, an emotional connector to his core; and the Lion, leading the way to the witches' castle. They needed the journey down the Yellow Brick Road to realize what was inside of them all along.

You have been dumped into an unfamiliar land, language you can barely interpret, and the idea of feeling optimistic or positive about seeing what you are made of is probably not on your radar. But the reality is this cancer is here now, so you might as well learn all the things you can during your own journey down the yellow brick road.

In the Wizard of Oz, the Lion represents your courage. The Lion is introduced later in the movie. He is the third friend that Dorothy meets on the Yellow Brick Road. He was trying with all of his might to intimidate Toto, the Tin Man and the Scare Crow. Fear is unruly and drives our anxiety every chance it gets. Dorothy learns to be firm. She slaps the Lion and demands he stops. Only in her firmness does the Lion show vulnerability, admitting he is scared of his own shadow. You must learn that fear is part of this scary journey in the thick of the forest. Fear is a natural part of the journey. You must learn to be in control of the fear and invite it along as part of your healing journey..

Taking control may take some very strong words, such as: "Stop talking about death. Stop saying this cancer is going to kill me. And for crying out loud quit wasting time on that false belief!" Others may think, "What did I do to deserve this?" This cancer is not your fault. If you want to keep up that underserving thought, just take a virtual walk through St. Jude's hospital for children or Google children with cancer. After you have taken that virtual tour, you tell me which one of those young vulnerable children caused his/her cancer? So, why do you think you are any different than any one of those vulnerable children?

Cancer happens. Cancer happens to everyone all around the world. Statistics told us in 2011 that 12.7 million people are diagnosed with cancer each year, and 7.6 million die from the disease. You did not have a choice, nor did you cause your disease. Your choice now is, how do you plan to live with this cancer. And the answer so far is: ACTION,

BREATH, and COURAGE. You are going to build a courageous heart and a disciplined mind. You are going to fight this with all your wisdom, strength, and courage. You are going to live your life now like you have never lived it before.

When you are so tired that you can't do anything but sit on the couch, you are going to turn off the T.V. and spend ten minutes meditating. Then you are going to read something positive. Then you are going to journal or color. Then you are going to drink some green tea or lemon water. Then you are going to take a nap. Next you are going to repeat the above until you have the strength to go for a walk for ten minutes. COURAGE is developed over a period of time. It is not a magic pill that you take and everything gets all better.

THREE HELPFUL PRACTICES:

1. **Read someone else's story that has been where you are.**

2. **Make an appointment with a psychotherapist, health coach, or spiritual director.**

3. **Watch movies where the heroine/hero win.**

DE-STRESS
LEARN TO TAKE CONTROL

Being diagnosed with cancer is a life changing event. Whether graduating from college or being diagnosed with a life-threatening illness, all life changing events are stressful. Stress is defined as an emotional strain from an adverse or demanding situation. And when you've been diagnosed with cancer, your whole body is under attack. Physically, an uninvited invasion enters your cells, and uses all of your physical resources and fighter cells to battle the invasion.

Now your mind is busy defending imaginary calamities, frightening day-time monsters, and night time sleep annihilators. Fear is often out of control, but you need to rise to the occasion and DE-STRESS. You need your energy and mental acuity to make wise decisions and move your set point back to a healthy self. Cancer is not what it used to be, but it is still serious business and must be dealt with aggressively.

I often ask my clients to tell me what they think his/ her stress level is like on a scale of 1-10, with 10 being extremely stressful. Unsurprising, I most likely hear the answer 8-10. But if I first ask the client to detail the stressors in his/her daily life, often I hear, "Well my life is not all that stressful." Asking someone to scale the amount of stress is less invasive than asking, "What is stressing you?" Of course, as a cancer patient you are stressed.

However, if you think back months ago before you knew, (probably the cancer was already there) how stressed were you on a scale of 1-10, you may have still answered 8-10. Life is stressful with work, family, adult responsibilities and so many details that must be managed.

As a society, we have been socialized to think this is normal and that there is something wrong with us if we can't handle all of it. The truth is that part of our job as human beings is to practice acts of DE-STRESSING everyday throughout the day.

You must learn to take control of your schedule and place self-help tools such as meditation, imagery, breathing, and relaxation into your daily schedule. These are not luxuries that you do when you are done with your to to-do list. These are life-saving necessities that you must put into action.

There are many DE-STRESSING tools in this book. The one thing to remember is that you do not have control over this disease, nor does it have control over you.

Control is over-rated and stressful in and of itself. It implies that we have done something wrong when something goes wrong. Our best attitude toward cancer is to become positive about the disease. It is here, it has presented us with a challenge, and we must prepare to work with the challenge in the best ways we know how. DE-STRESSING will help us be in a positive position to do what we must do to heal.

THREE HELPFUL PRACTICES:

1. **Practice your breathing exercises.**
2. **Work from a to do list.**
3. **Drink a nice organic herbal tea and be still inside.**

EVALUATE
PUT TOGETHER AN ACTION PLAN

What makes you want to live? Life can end up feeling like busy activity, one busy activity after another. When cancer comes along you are thrown into the business of surviving, a major part of surviving is the art of EVALUATION. Use this opportunity to EVALUATE who you are, what you want, and how you want to live your life daily. There are many benefits to sitting with yourself and musing over your life.

One way to EVALUATE in an organized way is to journal or make lists. Start with your story. Make time to sit with yourself and write down the story of your life up to this point. It can even be a creative story in third person. Let's call you "Destiny" for now. Begin with your birth. Destiny was born into a family of three sisters and two brothers. Destiny's dad was an accountant and mother was a nurse. You get my point.

You report the facts about yourself in third person. When you are finished writing your life up to the present, put the journaling away for a day or two and return to it as Destiny's inner counselor.

- **What advice do you have for Destiny?**
- **How has Destiny done so far?**
- **What about Destiny makes you proud and what make you disappointed?**
- **How would you EVALUATE Destiny's life so far?**

In this book, you are learning not only to accept the fact that cancer has come into your life, but that you can't change that reality.

You are learning to use this cancer as an opportunity to get more of what you want with the life you have by starting to EVALUATE what you like and don't like about your life.

You can change the pieces of your life that have annoyed you over the years. When you take responsibility to change the things you don't like, you come face to face with the question, "How important is this to me to change it?" Your mind makes up reasons that often have an unhappy storyline. If you don't discipline your thinking, your mind will gravitate to the negative and subtly remind you of the failures.

Now that you are a cancer patient, you may be reevaluating what is important to you. You may realize that you don't really need to change very much about who you really are or you become more accepting of the values and facts about you.

Are you kind, considerate, and helpful to others? How much is enough? See how tricky that is? There is always room for improvement. EVALUATION is a never-ending process, so you decide how much change is necessary and enough. Now put together an action plan and go for it!

THREE HELPFUL PRACTICES:

1. **Focus on only three priorities. I suggest health, relationships, and passion.**

2. **Be honest with what you want to change and why. A helpful question is: "If I change this, how will my life change for the better?**

3. **Keep a daily journal of who, what and how so you can reflect as you continue to EVALUATE.**

FUN
ALLOW YOURSELF AS MUCH FUN AS YOU CAN

What in the world is FUN about doctor's appointments, treatments, and intrusive medical procedures? FUN is simply defined as amusement, amusing, playful and enjoyable. The "H" word in this book is Happy. Happy is more of a state of being, whereas FUN is a moment in time that you are doing something that you enjoy and makes you smile. For instance, watching your favorite sports team play is a FUN time. Going to a movie that makes you laugh or suspends reality for a moment is FUN. Listening to music and moving your body can be FUN. Certainly, playing a family board game or a game of corn-hole can be FUN. Quilting can be fun.

Even when you are not battling for your life, FUN can be illusive in your normal day to day life. Often you are way too busy being too serious about too many things. Now, that life has seriously gotten your attention, one of the most important things we can do along the way is have FUN.

Take a moment with a paper and pencil and see if you can list five things (activities) that are FUN. It is harder than you think! Now, see if you can list three rules that prevent you from having FUN or having more FUN in your life.

Rules are internal limits you set on yourself for no reason except you feel like you should or should not do certain things. Maybe you believe having FUN is a waste of time. Maybe you believe you shouldn't have FUN because there is still laundry to do. Maybe you believe that you don't deserve to play like others because there is not enough money to have FUN. I bet it was not nearly as hard to list the rules around FUN as it was to list five things you can do to have FUN?

There is no better time to change your life and your belief system than right now. You only have the time you have right now. Time is precious and what better way to spend it than having some FUN. Google FUN activities and FUN things to do. Choose one FUN activity that is possible for you to accomplish right now. Maybe it something like taking the dog for a walk or as simple as picking up that novel you never finished. FUN is different for each of us. I can have FUN working a puzzle or going to the park and shooting baskets. FUN can be a family hike, bike ride, or just making fun pancakes for breakfast.

There will be many days that you may not feel like having FUN because of aching body parts or waves of nausea; but attitude is everything. It is important that you push the internal re-set button as often as possible and to allow yourself as much FUN as you can. You cannot look back at opportunities lost along the way. You cannot afford to feel sorry for you yourself and drop into despair.

It is important to your emotional health to find ways to find some FUN each day. Giving yourself a simple positive boost everyday can help you heal, feel better and maintain a healthier outlook as you continue your journey with cancer.

THREE HELPFUL PRACTICES:

1. **Google ways to have FUN today.**

2. **Write down FUN ideas when they pop up in your head or on your Facebook.**

3. **Be willing to break one of your rules you wrote down earlier.**

GAP

THE IN-BETWEEN SPACES YOU COME TO UNDERSTAND

I first heard about The Gap while listening to a dialogue between Pema Chodron (a Buddhist nun) and K.D. Lang (international vocal artist). The GAP is that in-between space where you come to experience the presence of "now." The GAP is that moment when you look up from a hiking path and notice the sky or the tree or the bird. It is that moment you smell the aroma of coffee brewing. The GAP is the moment where the ordinary becomes magical. The GAP is a sacred space within, when we realize we are part of the outer world.

It seems to me that as people living in the world of cancer, you can use the practice of the GAP regardless of where you are on the path. The GAP is a space within that allows you to breathe deeply from the inside out. As people experiencing cancer, life can become very ugly and painful as rancid smells and nauseating waves of emotion run askew inside the inner darkness. It is important that you do not live in the darkness. You must learn to explore the feelings of the darkness, breathe into it, and then release the darkness. The practice of the GAP is a tool to help you move past the darkness into the present moment.

Find something good and magical in the day. If you can't find magic in your day then create magic. If you are irritated with not getting the results you want with your health care, go and purchase some flowers. Yes, guys you too need to buy some flowers. Buying flowers for yourself as a male will magically transform you out of your social norm, "that flowers are for women." Take time to have a GAP moment with those flowers. Smell them, touch them and notice how each one is uniquely different from every other one. Have you ever noticed that no two roses are exactly alike? Notice the nuances in the shades of the colors, notice the stems. Notice each flower as you arrange it in the vase. These flowers traveled from rich fertile soil and were "harvested" for your delight. All cut flowers will die. But each flower has its own elegance, story, and purpose in your life today. The flower is here to bring you joy and to put a gentle smile on your face. Enjoying flowers is a GAP moment and you created it out of action and an idea.

As you learn to experience GAP moments, be the GAP in someone else's life today. Pick up the phone and call a friend and tell them how much they mean to you. Send a card to someone who needs a connection. Smile at the clerk in the grocery store and tell them, "I hope you have a really good day," as you look them in the eye. I imagine your health care team will respond to you more positively if you are practicing GAP moments in your life.

You are not cancer. You are not your disease. You are a person with many roles and facets to your life. Don't let cancer define you. Smile, spite of the cancer. Bring smiles to other people's lives. Make a difference today and you will be happier because you did.

THREE HELPFUL PRACTICES:

1. **Check out this live stream video: live.soundstrue.com/pemakdlang/.**

2. **Write down three GAP moments that you had today.**

3. **Do something out of the ordinary to create a unique GAP Moment.**

HAPPINESS
HOW TO MOVE
FORWARD

HAPPY is not usually a word that comes to mind when you have been diagnosed with cancer. HAPPY is a complicated word. Perhaps you have even felt discouraged over the years because you feel you are not as HAPPY as you want to be. Sometimes this is the case when we believe HAPPY is something outside of ourselves or "over the rainbow?"

Now you are diagnosed with cancer and there is nothing HAPPY about the diagnosis nor the treatment. However, HAPPINESS is not dependent on what is going on outside of you. HAPPINESS is an inside job. On a scale of 1-10, how would you rate your HAPPINESS prior to your diagnosis? 1 = not HAPPY at all to 10 = extremely HAPPY. Now, after your diagnosis, how do you rate your degree of HAPPINESS? Has this diagnosis made you unhappier than you were in the past, or are you just scared and anxious about all the unknown?

HAPPINESS is not an illusion but neither is it a destination. HAPPINESS is mostly about your attitude towards life and what you believe.

Your beliefs may be very unconscious because you haven't really thought about them. Perhaps, you have been operating from a "less-than HAPPY" state of being.

Maybe you believe that HAPPINESS is a matter of luck or something only rich people obtain. As a result, you set yourself up to never quite achieve HAPPINESS because you believe HAPPINESS is based on circumstances. HAPPINESS is not about your circumstances. However, HAPPINESS is based on your attitude toward your circumstances.

You cannot change the fact that you have a cancer diagnosis. If you accept the reality of that diagnosis then you are free to ask yourself, "Since I have cancer, what is my best attitude toward this disease?" Yes, the emotions around this diagnosis are complicated. You will experience anger, fear, sadness and somedays despair. Those are emotions. You don't want to get stuck in those emotions, you want to let the emotions move through your being. It is very healthy to experience each and every complicated emotion.

Once the emotions have been acknowledged, ask yourself, "what do I need to focus on to help my body heal?"

Anger is to be expected. Cancer has interrupted your life. Accepting your anger, writing about it and letting it go is necessary for you to create HAPPY. Ignoring complicated emotions such as anger leads to unhappiness. Accepting, working with, and moving on when complicated emotions show up is the inner work that will help you heal.

If you change your attitude and accept that HAPPINESS is an inside job, then you can examine your beliefs about HAPPINESS and redirect the beliefs that no longer serve you to a more positive focus. Beliefs can be changed and emotions need to stay fluid, moving in and out like the tide of the ocean. Without waves the ocean would not be nearly as appealing, without emotions you become stale, dull, and uninteresting. With a full range of different emotions, you have the ability to move toward that HAPPY space inside you. Your attitude is everything.

THREE HELPFUL PRACTICES:

1. **Imagine a safe place and create all that you need to be in that safe place and experience HAPPY.**

2. **Journal your feelings. Treat your feelings as friends. Get to know you anger so that you can heal it.**

3. **When you are feeling unhappy, examine what the unhappiness is trying to tell you. Listen to that small voice and give it what it needs.**

IMAGERY
HOW TO FIND & CREATE HEALTHY IMAGES

Finding and creating healthy images in your brain really can help your body move forward in positive ways. Your brain is like a computer. You are in charge of programing it with the software that will help you heal. Often referred to as guided imagery or creative visualization, IMAGERY is an important tool to help your body and mind connect and speak to each other.

If you look at the cover of my book, *In A Moment's Notice*, you will see a Tiger and a Labyrinth. I used the imagery of the Tiger coming into my body and eating the mutant cells every day. All of these years later, I still send my tiger into my body to consume those cells daily. We all have rogue mutant cancer cells in our bodies and the goal is not to let those rogue cells get together and have a tumor building party! An important key in imagery work is that it must be believable to you. If you don't believe imagery has the healing powers to destroy your mutant cells, the imagery will not be as helpful.

Discovering what images you want to create to help you walk this path, it is most important that you find a believable image, an image in which you can create a relationship. My Tiger came to me in a lucid dream state in the middle of the night. I prayed for an image to help me through this journey. I played with some ideas like water, warriors, and other types of characters, but nothing stuck or spoke to me.

To find your very own IMAGERY you might ask yourself, what characters from mythology, movies, stories, or even sports figures speak to you? By speaking to you, I mean, allowing yourself to completely engage in thinking, feeling, experiencing what it would be like to have Babe Ruth knock those cells right out of the ballpark. Or imagine creating a magical waterfall that can rinse the cancer cells out of your body each day. Imagine feeling eager to go to that beautiful internal waterfall, stand under it letting it make you whole again. With a little help from your creative self, the mind can create the believable circumstances that allow you to transport yourself to your own healing garden.

This idea of using images to work with cancer cells is not new. I learned to trust this imagery work from working with a former client. She was diagnosed with non-treatable colon cancer. When she came to see me after her diagnosis, she brought me the book, **Getting Well Again** by Carl Simonton, and told me she was using the image of Snow White and Seven Dwarfs to go through her body and mop out the cancer cells. She was a first -

grade teacher, so that imagery and the structure of twenty minutes three times a day worked for her.

Since then, research on imagery has shown it is not so important to do it twenty-minutes at a time, but rather doing it often and making sure that you are participating in a believable way with your image doing the healing work. Enjoy discovering your image.

THREE HELPFUL PRACTICES:

1. **Google guided imagery and listen to some of the free audio feeds on line.**

2. **Make a list of some images that might work for you.**

3. **Practice mindfully using those images in your mind's eye and see which one seems to be the right one for you.**

JOURNALING
CREATE MEANING OUT OF TRAUMA

The importance of JOURNALING, often dismissed or overlooked, is not just diary keeping. JOURNALING is an avenue of self-expression, reflection, and record keeping. It allows the emotions we carry to flow through our being. Right now, you are flooded with a variety of strong emotions and fearful thoughts and being able to get those feelings out and expressed rather than suppressing them directly impacts your happiness, health and wellbeing. As a matter of fact, JOURNALING is so impactful as a tool for healing that research is being done on the various aspects of writing, such as the research conducted by J. Pennebaker and J. Smyth, who have found some amazing health benefits:

1. **Journaling strengthens immune cells, called T-lymphocytes.**

2. **Journaling reduces physical symptoms and suppressed emotions adds to physical disease.**

3. **Journaling helps clients find and create meaning out of his or her trauma.**

Many of you get scared or intimidated by the look of a blank page starring back at you. Others don't consider the effort worth the reward, but I am inviting you to see your JOURNAL as your friend and confidant. The empty pages are an invitation for you to share your story and feelings freely.

Having a diagnosis of cancer is like being hit on the head with the window from the Wizard of Oz and finding yourself in a strange land where flying monkeys taunt you, a wicked witch wants your dog (intuition) and your sparkly red shoes (a symbol of your inner magic).
Writing every day, even if it is a one word entry such as "hopeless," will help you keep track of your journey and provide you with stepping stones along the way.

Yes, writing just one word on a blank page is helpful. Another way of JOURNALING is to color. Draw a big circle in the middle of your blank page and choose three colors that represent what you are feeling right now. Fill in the circle with those colors. Choose a comforting or nurturing color and color all of the outside of the circle with that color as a way of soothing those inner feelings.

Another way to get that blank page to warm up is to write letters. You can write letters to yourself, your God, your friends and family members. Letter writing as JOURNALING is safe because you are never going to send what your write so you can express yourself freely. You will not have to edit what you say. You can tell it like it is. If you think a friend has let you down in this process, journal a letter to that friend. If your regrets are bothering you, JOURNAL yourself a letter. Write positive letters of thanks and gratitude too.

Having a safe and private place to write your most intimate feelings is also important. In my book, A-Z Mindful Practices, I suggest that you put a note on front of your journal that reads: "This is private material. Please do not trespass on my privacy. Breast Cancer has stolen a lot from me and violated me. Please do not do the same."

Remember, you are in survivor's mode and the brain is not able to process all that you are experiencing. That is why your JOURNAL becomes your unconditionally loving friend. A year after treatment, re-read it and you will be surprised how much you went through on this journey. If you have never journaled before, now is a great time to start. If you are a regular journal writer, then make sure you keep it up now.

THREE HELPFUL PRACTICES:
1. **Don't overthink what you are JOURNALING. Just start writing.**

2. **Read this article on the health benefits of journaling. http://www.apa.org/monitor/jun02/ writing.aspx**

3. **Write or color something every day, even if it is one word.**

KINDNESS
TRAIN YOUR MIND
TO BE POSITIVE

Now more than ever you need KINDNESS. What is KINDNESS and how do you maintain it when you feel so vulnerable? The Dali Lama says, "Kindness is my religion." KINDNESS is an attitude of gentleness toward others and yourself. When you are fighting for your life there can be quite a bit of chatter in your head that can dampen your spirit and mood.

Often, you can hear yourself saying things inside of your head like, "You really screwed up this time. This is bad." Or "No one understands me and how scared I am." Maybe, "The doctor doesn't care. A paycheck is all that he/she wants," the list goes on. I am sure you can add three unkind statements without even trying. The truth is, our mind does this to us every day. It is easier to be negative than positive. That is why we must train our mind to practice KINDNESS.

First, you must give yourself permission to be KIND to yourself. You need KINDNESS now more than ever. You must learn to say things to yourself like, "Even though this is hard right now, you can do this" and "It is okay to ask for help." My guess is that these positive statements do not come easy to you. I also imagine that it is more natural for you to say kind statements to others before you say them to yourself. I want you to start with yourself. In Pema Chodron's book, The Places That Scare You, she shares a Buddhist Loving Kindness Practice. The practice always starts with the self. For example,

> *"May I experience loving kindness and the root of loving kindness. May my (most important person in your life) experience loving kindness and the root of loving kindness. May my friend experience loving kindness and the root of loving kindness. May (a stranger like the store clerk) experience loving kindness and the root of loving kindness. May the person (I dislike or who is difficult) experience loving kindness and the root of loving kindness. May all the above experience loving kindness and the root of loving kindness. May all beings experience loving kindness and the root of loving kindness. "*

This is a great map to help you start practicing KINDNESS today. Use it often throughout the day. Make it a mantra when you are feeling overwhelmed or upset. Use it when your medical team or family members appear to be done with this journey of yours. Or when you need to give yourself the gift of rest.

You can never have too much KINDNESS. You can never be too KIND to any person. The people in your life who are difficult need your KINDNESS the most. It is possible to change the whole atmosphere in a medical office, a bus stop, or your chemo-room with acts of KINDNESS because All emotions create more emotions. Observe people around you and notice what happens. An angry person usually gets treated with anger in return. A sad person is usually avoided by others. A happy person creates interest from others. A KIND person may get rebuffed by anger but that is not the rule of thumb. The rule of thumb is that most people will treat you with the same respect or lack of respect you treat them. Practice KINDNESS today.

THREE HELPFUL PRACTICES:

1. **Use the above mindfulness tool often, every day.**

2. **Practice looking into someone's eyes and smiling.**

3. **Be KIND to yourself with your self-talk.**

LABYRINTH
TOOL FOR INNER CONFIDENCE

The LABYRINTH is an underutilized tool that can be used as a walking meditation. Meditation, mindfulness, and spirituality are like a three-legged stool; each leg carries a specific weight allowing you to balance perfectly. A labyrinth helps you do all three.

Cancer is not something that you can face on your own. You need a team of skilled medical professionals, a cheering squad of family and friends. You will need a variety of resources and tools that can help you cope with all that you are going through. Most importantly, you need an inner relationship with yourself and your spirituality. The labyrinth is a great tool to help you connect to your quiet inner self and the spirit.

The labyrinth is a great tool to help you connect to your quiet inner self and the spirit. The LABYRINTH is not a religious tool and it is not associated with any particular religion. The symbol of the LABYRINTH is found all around the world and dates to medieval times. Recently, there has a been a resurgence of the LABYRINTH coming to life in churches, hospitals, schools, parks, and prisons throughout the world. People who walk the LABYRINTH report different experiences, but mainly there is a report of an inner shift that results in more peace, inner confidence, resolve, getting clear, and letting go.

When I was wrapping up my first experience with cancer treatment, I made a commitment to walk the LABYRINTH once a week for a year. During that year, I fell in love with this symbol and have chosen to share it with you, so that you might find peace and patience in this long journey with cancer. Even though one day a doctor may tell you that you are cancer free, you will never be able to go back to that secure immortality that you had prior to your diagnosis.

Here is a simple guide to help you as you develop your own relationship with the LABYRINTH. Each labyrinth has one path into a center and same path out again. All you do is put one foot in front of the other. As you stand at the opening you will want to set your intention. For instance, today you walk for healing or peace, or comfort. As you begin putting one foot in front of the other you may notice that your brain lets go of its chatter and the anxiety and fear begin to trail at your feet. As you continue the path you may notice the peace and comfort that the walk has to offer. As you arrive in the center, there you will spend as much or as little time as you need having an internal conversation, while continuing to let go but also receiving what you need. As you walk out the same path that you entered, you will focus on returning to your day to day life with what you need. As you exit, you can turn and thank the path for being there for you today. Each time you walk a LABYRINTH you may have a different experience.

On some walks you may not notice experiencing anything at all. Learning to trust the process is part of the practice of a walking meditation. LABYRINTH as a walking meditation is a ritual, a symbol, and a time apart from the ordinary to practice non-ordinary means of communication with Spirit. The LABYRINTH is a tool that will help us do that in one space.

It is even possible to walk a labyrinth with your finger. There are several styles of labyrinths and after you google them you may find one style feels better to you than another. Print of a copy of labyrinth that you like and use your finger to follow the path into the center and back out again. You can purchase hand-held labyrinths on line and below is a link to help you find a walking labyrinth near you. Give it a try and see for yourself how the labyrinth speaks to you.

THREE HELPFUL PRACTICES:

1. **Go to www.labyrinthlocator.com and enter your zip to find a labyrinth near you.**

2. **Google where to buy finger labyrinths to use one when it is not possible to walk one.**

3. **Read about labyrinths and their history.**

MINDFULNESS
TRAIN YOUR BRAIN
TO OVERCOME
CIRCUMSTANCES

MINDFULNESS is a word that you most likely have heard before. It is a word used in psychological and spiritual literature. But, MINDFULNESS is more than a word. MINDFULNESS is a practice of attention. MINDFULNESS is as simple as switching your attention from the chatter inside of your head to the outside world. Pay attention to what you see, feel, think, hear, smell and intuit. When you receive the scary words, "You have cancer," your world closes in on you. Your mind runs helter-skelter, bringing up every image and horror story you have ever heard about people with cancer. You might be saying, or even screaming right now, "I don't have time to pay attention or to learn to meditate. Didn't you hear me? I have cancer!"

Yes, I hear you loud and clear, and I have been where you are before. MINDFULNESS has been a tool that has saved me from my fear repeatedly. I have been afraid, terrorized, and confused by this big bad word, cancer. However, I could not stay there; and my hope is that this small book on MINDFULNESS, words will help re-direct you and challenge you to drop the story line of fear and adopt a new way of looking at this scary word.

Remember in the Wizard of Oz, Dorothy slaps the cowardly lion to get him to stop intimidating and scarring her friends? When she slapped the Lion, the Lion calmed down. MINDFULNESS is a way of calming your lion down without having to slap yourself. Being mindful does take discipline; training your mind to think about what you want instead of scaring you to death is a challenge and it takes lots of repetitive practice. You never fail at MINDFULNESS. You just keep training the mind to see, think, feel, and reflect on the positive. MINDFULNESS is a repetitive discipline.

There is nothing hard about MINDFULNESS. There is nothing bulky or clumsy about MINDFULNESS. This book is designed to make MINDFULNESS simple. It is a short book of twenty-six words written to redirect your mind from fear to hope. By focusing on these words, you will learn to direct your experience to hope, and the joy of hope even when you are in a very difficult and chaotic time in your life. You probably have never had cancer before, but you have had plenty of different types of scary times in your life up to now. You overcame those circumstances and you will get through this too. My goal is to help you get through this in creative and meaningful ways that build up your emotional muscles of courage, strength, and hope.

Train your brain, like Dorothy did in the Wizard of Oz, and do not let it your anxiety take you off your path of recovery. Choose to close your eyes and focus on seeing your body get healthy again, watch your body in your mind's eye do what it used to do and do it effortlessly. Use the imagery you created to assist you on this journey. MINDFULNESS as a repetitive practice is a space that you set aside and spend time focusing, reflecting, remembering and creating a story of health, vibrancy, and hope that will assist you along this journey.

THREE HELPFUL PRACTICES:
1. **Staying in the present is the key to grounded mindfulness.**
2. **Read short articles on MINDFULNESS practices.**
3. **Set a timer for 3 minutes and practice MINDFULNESS practices each day. Build from 3 minutes to 5 minutes and move on from there.**

NOTICE
TOOLS FOR CHOOSING HOW TO SPEND YOUR TIME

NOTICE can be a verb or a noun depending on the context of how it is being used. Imagine waking up this morning and having a handwritten notice on your pillow that says, "Your life will expire in thirty-days, make the most of it." Now that is a NOTICE! You now have a choice to make. In one sense, you are one of the lucky ones, you received the NOTICE of your time on earth. You can choose to be angry and distressed that you have only thirty days left, or you can choose to focus on what matters most to you in the next thirty days. NOTICE I said you get to choose what and how you want to spend your time?

I used the word NOTICE as a verb in that sentence to draw your attention to the word "you," and thus it is your choice how you want to spend the remaining time. Maybe you want to fly off to see the Amalfi Coast in Italy or jump from an airplane? Perhaps your family wants you to come for a visit and spend your last thirty days with them? When you have two conflicting choices, you can choose to make it a win-win for you, or if that is not possible, clearly make it a win for you. A NOTICE is an announcement of something important that should not be ignored whether it be in verb or noun form. Take NOTICE and get a move on.

Yes, in one way the cancer diagnosis has placed you on NOTICE. You will NOTICE life differently now, but the goal is to keep the NOTICE alive. Live more fully because you are aware of your immortality. NOTICE sunrises and sunsets in new ways. Don't take that hummingbird for granted. Instead, enjoy NOTICING how it can fly backwards as easily as it flies forward. Take time to slow down and NOTICE your environment. Pick up a favorite knick-knack and truly look at it. Where/how did you get it? What about the object made you fall in love with it? Does the object have a message for you? What is it?

Spend some quiet moments with yourself and notice what comes up inside. Let your emotions come to the surface and greet them with a curious mind. What are you feeling on the surface? What feeling might be underneath the surface? Is there something you are not feeling? NOTICING your emotions and making room for each of them, the good, the bad, and the ugly is very important to your mental health. Ignoring your emotions can lead you into dangerous places.

Let your emotions become your friends by providing you intel about yourself to help you make important decisions. Life is more vibrant and meaningful each day when you take the time to NOTICE the little and big things. You can learn to marvel at the magic and mystery that is always around you as though you are seeing it for the first time.

1. **NOTICE the strangers in your life. Look the clerk in the eye; smile at your technician.**

2. **NOTICE your breath. Breathe more consciously and appreciate the breaths you are taking.**

3. **Find time to NOTICE the small things that people do for you and be thankful.**

OPPORTUNITY

HOW TO MAKE YOUR LIFE MORE MEANINGFUL

The mind is a beautiful thing or, like a wild-stallion, refuses to be trained. Stallions are majestic to look at but they could kill you in a heart-beat if they are not well trained. Your mind may do the same if you do not train it to do what you need right now. Yes, cancer, a horrible disease, often viewed as a scary illness because cancer treatment is notorious for how rough it is on the body.

Thus, your mind, which is where your perceptions; consciousness; memory; judgements; and thoughts take place, is the key to rallying your whole-self during this time.

Seeing this time as an OPPORTUNITY may pose a challenge, however, a necessary mental adjustment to make it through this time with a positive attitude.

I understand that it is hard to see cancer as an opportunity, especially since the treatment can be brutal and the possibility that it is terminal is frightening. It is true, that I am asking you to see this as an opportunity to make positive decisions. Some people do not get a wake-up call or a pink slip warning them of what is ahead. Some of you have had people slip out of your lives overnight through accidents, heart attacks or other disasters that swept them from your lives. Seeing cancer as an OPPORTUNITY to take care of business, change the unhappy areas of your life, and create more of what you want is important. Our attitudes and our thoughts must be trained to focus on the positive parts of this journey. If you focus only on the negative parts or how hard it is, you could survive your cancer and end up being bitter. That choice would be sad. I am inviting you to focus on what OPPORTUNITIES this wake-up call has for you in the midst of your fear.

Seizing this diagnosis as an OPPORTUNITY is not at all easy nor simple. It is a practice in the mind that requires you to be in charge. Do you know what your real beliefs are about your cancer? Write a journal letter to your cancer and tell it what you think and feel about it. Re-read that letter in a day or so and you may discover that you have a belief that you have cancer because of something you feel guilty about in your past. Ah, there you have it. Guilt serves no useful purpose. It is an invader in your mind telling you what you should have done or not done instead. Guilt hangs around for years, nagging and complaining and wearing your immune system down.

Cancer is an OPPORTUNITY to deal with those past feelings of guilt and let go of them once and for all. Training your mind to say, "No," "Stop," when hurtful thoughts pass through is so important to your healing. But you just can't put up a stop sign, you must redirect your thoughts. If you feel guilty about twenty-six things in your past then list twenty-six things that you have done well, or contributed to your life or someone else's life.

Today you are still alive and therefore you have the OPPORTUNITY to change things in your life that are not working for you. This is an OPPORTUNITY to take inventory of what you want in your life and what you want to get rid of in your life. Keep a journal, make lists, write down your night-time dreams, and focus on getting better every day. This is an OPPORTUNITY to practice some of the tools in this book and make your life more meaningful.

Living in the present is one of the best OPPORTUNITIES that cancer gives you. Yesterday is gone and the future is uncertain, thus making the most of today is the OPPORTUNITY to make your life count again and again.

THREE HELPFUL PRACTICES:

1. **Inventory your mind. What things do you feel guilty about? What nags at you about your past? Write those things down in a list or as stories.**

2. **Make a focus list or stories of wonderful and positive things you have done with your life.**

3. **Think of your mind as a beautiful stallion that is trained to do what you need it to do: focus on the OPPORTUNITY.**

PATIENCE
HOW TO FOCUS YOUR ATTENTION

PATIENCE is the friend we all need during this time of cancer treatment and in the years ahead of us. PATIENCE is the friend you will need on your journey. What is PATIENCE?

If you google PATIENCE, you may be disappointed in the ambiguity in the definition. Think about PATIENCE as the quality of steadiness, calmness, and focused attention. Do not be distracted by things that go wrong. Each day provides us with ample opportunities to be impatient, cranky, agitated, and snarky. The goal is to practice the qualities of PATIENCE instead. Be kind, take a breath, pause, and remind yourself that you have choices about how you respond to those around you.

The lack of PATIENCE will make you feel shame, regret, and guilt. When you blow up at someone or show your "ugly side," you are the one that ends up feeling rotten about it later. Guilt is a destructive emotion and costs you many wasted positive experiences. Thus, it is very important to practice PATIENCE with yourself, first. You are not perfect and no matter how hard you try, you are never going to be perfect. Learn to be kind and steadfast with yourself when you have a melt-down or an ugly moment. Stop, take a few breathes and notice your environment by switching your attention to the colors in the room. Breathe and list what you see in your environment. For instance, if you are in your kitchen, notice the colors on the walls and name the refrigerator, stove and oven. This distraction technique stops your brain from battering you or battering others with your outrage. Breathe again. Close your eyes and breathe some more. Maybe take a walk around the yard outside or a walk in the parking lot if you are in a public place. While walking, name what you see, such as the gravel, a tree, a bird. Breathe again.

When you can say to yourself, "I am truly sorry that I reacted that way and I forgive myself for my outburst," then you are ready to go back and apologize to the person or persons for your reaction. You must learn to make things right with yourself first.

Learning to walk in self-forgiveness and positive self-care will help you be gentle with others. Being gentle with others while being mean and angry with yourself will make you cranky and irritable. That behavior will drive others away. Having cancer is not permission to be rude, cranky, or agitated towards others.

Practicing PATIENCE is work and doing it on a moment by moment basis will gift you with the following three blessings: One, you will feel a sense of positive self-esteem. Also, you will truly learn to like yourself. Finally, you will be a person people want to be around.

PATIENCE is an attribute you can learn. If you say, "I am just not a PATIENT person," that is a limiting and maybe even a lazy belief. You can learn PATIENCE, but it takes practice. Piano players and star athletes must practice every day to keep their skills competitive. You must learn to practice PATIENCE every day to be a happy human being. Make it game and go out and be magical with your PATIENCE.

THREE HELPFUL PRACTICES:

1. **Always take time to breath.**

2. **Try smiling when you are angry or agitated.**

3. **Use techniques in this book, such as journaling or mindfulness.**

QUESTION
DO NOT BE AFRAID
TO USE YOUR VOICE

Yes, question everything. Rilke the poet wrote, "Be patient toward all that is unsolved in your heart and try to love the question themselves. Do not now seek the answers which cannot be given you because you would not be able to live them. And the point is, to live everything. Live the questions now. Perhaps you will then gradually, without noticing it, live along some distant day into the answer." Thus, to question is to be alive.

Critical thinking and QUESTIONING is the key to helping yourself on this journey. Keep track of your journey, doctor's appointments, testing and progress.

Use a different color of pen to write down questions. Do not be afraid to use your voice with your doctor and to ask anything you want to ask. There are no dumb questions. Doctors are trained to only give information that he or she is asked about. Thus, they operate from a don't ask-don't tell policy. If you want to know your prognosis, the general rule of thumb is that you will have to ask. If your doctor says, "we will have to wait and see," and if that is not good enough for you ask, "what are the statistics for a cancer like mine?" You may have to say, "This is my life and I believe I have the right to know what the odds are." Others of you will not want to know the answer to that question. Doctors for the most part will honor that don't ask don't tell policy.

QUESTIONS THAT ARE IMPORTANT ARE:

- What will this test tell us?
- What possible reactions could I have to this drug?
- There are several drugs available for this, do you mind sharing why you are choosing this one?
- What can I do to help myself through this journey?
- Are there clinical trials available?
- Are there resources or reading materials that will help me?
- If this were your family member what would you tell them?
- As you read and think write your questions down, so that you remember to ask them.

Get curious and stay curious about this journey. Curiosity generates QUESTIONS. Document your symptoms, changes in your body, and ask the doctor about those things that you are observing. Do not be afraid to google your questions, just DO NOT take the google answers as relevant medical information.

However, googling can help you ask new questions. Your doctor has hundreds of other patients, it is impossible for him or her to be prepared for all your questions, but asking him or her to get back to you is also an option. By asking questions you become more alert, aware, and alive. The answers are constantly changing. Cancer research is bringing new information every month. Question, explore, and discover living into whatever answers may come your way. If no answers come, the risk of asking is still well worth the effort because the experiences along the way make all possibilities meaningful.

Whether the question is Who, What, How, When or Why, most all questions are important. However, there is one question I want you to put out of your mind, "Why did this happen to me?" The right question is "Now that this cancer is here, what can I do about it and what are my option?

THREE HELPFUL PRACTICES:
1. **Write down at least five questions you want to ask.**

2. **Examine what feelings/emotions/thoughts come up about your right to ask questions.**

3. **What questions do you not want to ask? Why? What could change if you asked those scary questions?**

REGRETS
CREATING A
PATH TOWARDS JOY

Life is too short for REGRETS. However, REGRETS are real, and you must find a way to resolve them and move from REGRETS to joy. REGRETS are the things in life that you are disappointed about, feel remorse or sadness about because you did something you wish you had not done. All of us have regrets. In order, to resolve or work through REGRETS you must face them head on. You cannot continue to avoid or bury them. Avoidance steals your joy. Even though you may be trying to go on as is if everything is just great, inside is a gnawing sadness that just won't go away. Maybe you even find yourself walking down the REGRET lane in the middle of the night because you keep avoiding it during the day.

Make a list of your REGRETS, but before you begin your list of REGRETS let's have a little pep talk.

There are big REGRETS and little REGRETS. Everyone one of us has a list of each. It is easiest to practice with the little REGRETS first. What is the difference, you ask? Little Regrets are things that we wish were different, such as wishing that you had said good-by to the neighbor before you moved and then they died before you "got around to-it." You were not that close to the neighbor, but she was a widow and all alone. A little act of kindness made her day and helped her feel connected. You ignored your intuitive side to go knock on her door and let her know the moving truck was coming today. That memory makes you sad but it does not change your life or your path toward joy.

Big REGRETS are life changing events from your past. Perhaps you said a hateful thing to a loved one and the loved one never got a chance to return home. Perhaps you were not paying attention and someone else was physically hurt by your carelessness. Perhaps you were hurt or permanently injured because of your own careless act. The reality is, each of us has done careless things in non-malicious ways and lived to pay the consequences of those actions.

What is important now is that you find a space within you to forgive yourself and stop returning to this dead-end street. What was done in the past cannot be changed now.

What can you do about it now? If there is a letter you can write to apologize, do it! Do not delay. If there is a phone call you can make, make it right now before you finish this reading. Procrastination leads to defeat. Clean out your REGRETS.

Practice a mantra that says, "may I be free from REGRETS and free from the root of REGRET." Say it over and over, again and again. Keep saying it until you make inside of you to truly be free of REGRET.

1. **Make a list of little REGRETS and an action plan to let them go.**

2. **Make a list of big REGRETS and an action plan to release them.**

3. **You may need the help of a psychotherapist, spiritual director, or coach for this one.)**

4. **Ask for forgiveness when necessary.**

SHAME
TOOLS TO HELP WITH ANGER & SHAME

Over the course of my career I have dedicated a tremendous amount of time studying and writing about SHAME. SHAME is a word that we are ashamed of, and spend our energy avoiding. The simplest definition of shame, "the interruption of positive affect" comes from the work of Silvan Tomkins. Cancer interrupts your positive feelings about life in big ways. You were busy living your daily life and then without any introduction or announcement, cancer arrived and interrupted everything. Rationally, you know that you have nothing to be ashamed of because cancer is a disease that happens to many people. Some survive it. Some die from it. But SHAME has nothing to do with rational thought.

Tomkins work speaks about the Compass of Shame. The Compass of Shame demonstrates that most people have one of four reactions to SHAME when it interrupts our positive life. Those reactions are 1.) attack self 2.) attack other 3.) avoid 4.) withdraw. What do you observe that you have done since your heard those words, "you have cancer?" Are you blaming yourself? Are you blaming someone else, like God? Have you chosen to ignore your diagnosis and pretend it does not exist? Or, have you closed your doors to others and taken on this battle as your battle alone to fight. None of the above options are going to be helpful to you getting through this diagnosis. SHAME left to its own destruction is crippling to the mind, body and spirit.

You have some wonderful tools in this book to help you cope with SHAME. Journaling and Imagery are two of the most important tools. The goal is to practice more positive actions and eliminate as many negative many actions and thoughts as possible. This is what Tomkins calls the Blueprint of Living. Perhaps, before cancer, you were not conscious of your thoughts, feelings, and actions. However, now that cancer is at your door it does change your level of awareness and consciousness.

Another way to frame SHAME is from a Jungian viewpoint of the Shadow. The Shadow is an archetype. For the most part the Shadow is alive and well in your unconscious self. Maybe you have tried to change things that have not been working for you to no avail. It is your Shadow side that sabotages your positive actions and keeps you trapped in the same old behavior. Carl Jung says we must learn to accept our dark side, the part of us that tricks us and keeps us trapped. By acknowledging that your Shadow side exists and needs you to practice kindness toward it then you are on your way to transforming the Shadow into a productive part of your life.

Do not waste your valuable time twisted up in SHAME, anger, and regrets. Cancer is here. Acknowledge it. Dialogue with the cancer and allow it to tell you the story of how it came into being and what it needs from you now that it is here. Giving voice to your cancer will help dissipate the SHAME of having it. When you move toward your cancer then you move out of SHAME. Tell your story, use you voice, and become visible. Those are the trinity of healing.

THREE HELPFUL PRACTICES:

1. **Journal your honest feelings about having cancer.**

2. **Share your cancer story with others, maybe a cancer support group.**

3. **Find something to enjoy each day.**

TALK
LEARN HOW TO ASK FOR WHAT YOU NEED

As a psychologist, I understand the benefits of TALKING about things, especially TALKING about emotions. I also understand how difficult it is to TALK about emotions, because TALKING about things that you feel, believe, or think can make you feel incredibly vulnerable. But now, more than ever before, it is of upmost importance to learn to TALK about what is going on inside of you.

In the story of the Wizard of Oz, Dorothy needed to TALK about her fears of Toto being taken away. No one on the farm had time to listen to what she needed so desperately to say. When Dorothy landed in Oz, she immediately had people to talk with by making friends with the Scare Crow, Tin Man, and Lion along the Yellow Brick Road. It would have been a very lonely journey without her friends. When I teach the Metaphors of the Wizard of Oz in a workshop, I teach that those three characters are part of our inside-self. In order to heal ourselves, we must make friends with these parts that feel unintelligent, unlovable, and afraid. As a person with cancer, I am sure you have those feelings. It is important to dialogue with those inner parts of yourself; but it is also very important to TALK to real people outside of yourself.

Your friends and family members are not perfect and may at times remind you of Dorothy's busy Aunt Em or distracted uncles. Be patient with yourself and with them, but do not become invisible or a martyr. Find one or two people that are willing to listen to your concerns, fears, hopes, and dreams. Use your voice and ask for what you need. Tell your friends or family member that you need to have a few trusted travelers to make this journey alongside of you. Ask them if they are willing to be present for thirty minutes a week to listen while you process your journey. Ask them to help you be accountable to do your best job facing this cancer. Ask them to be willing to comfort you when you are hurting; to encourage you to take one more step and listen to you while you try to figure out your way. Ask them to be honest with you and tell them it is okay to set boundaries with you.

Other folks who might be helpful to talk to are psychologists, counselors, social workers, or clergy. If you live in a bigger city you will have support groups available to you. Your oncologist can supply you with a list of support groups they recommend. If you live in a rural area or feel too fatigued to commute to a support group, you can google "cancer support groups" on-line and discover some resources available to you. Even if you are shy, give a support group a try because sharing your feelings with people who have been there can be tremendously helpful and nourish your soul.

TALK therapy has proven to be one of the most effective tools of psychology. Don't bottle up your emotions: bottled emotions harm your healthy cells. Chronic stress weakens your immune system. Now, more than ever, you need your body to receive everything it needs to return to a healthy state of being. TALK, TALK and TALK some more.

THREE HELPFUL PRACTICES:

1. **Practice using your voice to ask for what you need. Write it letter form in your journal first.**

2. **Choose at least one person you would like to ask to be available to you as a trusted companion during this time.**

3. **List your reasons for not talking to someone and ask yourself, "What do I have to lose at this important time in my life?"**

UBUNTU
HOW TO OFFER
YOURSELF & OTHERS
SELF-ASSURANCE

Sometime ago there was a post on FB of children sitting in a circle and creating another circle by touching their feet together with outstretched legs. The story was about UBUNTU. UBUNTU is an African word that means human kindness in a very progressive sense. These children were told that candy was beneath a tree and the child who got there first won all the candy. Instead of running off to the candy, the children reached for each other and ran together holding hands for the candy. They explained to the reporter that it is not kind for one to be happy and the rest to be sad. UBUNTU is a word that has woven itself deep within the African culture inclusive of its socialistic politics.

This deep equality of UBUNTU brings people together on the same playground and motivates them to work together for the good of the whole. How do you practice UBUNTU in your society and community, even if some are strangers or they look and act differently than you? Desmond Tutu writes in 1999, "A person with UBUNTU is open and available to others, affirming of others, does not feel threatened that others are able and good, based from a proper self-assurance that comes from knowing that he or she belongs in a greater whole and is diminished when others are humiliated, or diminished, when others are tortured or oppressed." The stranger next door is your brother or your sister so practice UBUNTU toward him or her. Let UBUNTU exude from your heart every day of this journey.

Diving deeper into the meaning of UBUNTU is the global knowledge of interdependence. As the children said, "it is not kind for one to be happy and the rest to be sad." The journey through cancer will have many sad moments. You will have the experience of sitting together with other cancer patients in chemotherapy together. Let your eyes meet his or her eyes. See them with "soft or kind" eyes. You are in this boat together doing the best you can. You are interdependent on each other. Your smile and soft eyes softens his or her experience making it more palatable and more hopeful along the way. It encourages those sitting around you. They come to rely on the fact, if you can do this so can they. You receive hope and courage from other chemotherapy patients too.

You might have an experience where someone you have engaged with does not return for the rest of his or her chemo. You may come to know that he or she has been taken by cancer. This news will make you afraid. It will make you wonder, "what about me?" This news will also make you sad and maybe for a little while, less willing to make eye contact and practice UBUNTU opportunities. As the book points out, none of us are getting out of this life alive and death is a part of life. Don't let fear strip you of your UBUNTU opportunities. You do have right now and right now is good-enough to make a difference in your life and the life of those that you are interdependent with. Let's go get the candy together and have some amazing experiences along the way. Life is better lived together and not alone. I invite you to step into the circle of UBUNTU and move forward.

THREE HELPFUL PRACTICES:

1. **Practice looking people in the eye with soft-kind eyes.**

2. **Read THE BOOK OF JOY by the Dali Lama and Desmond Tutu.**

3. **Do something to help someone out today.**

VULNERABILITY

HOW TO CULTIVATE
COMFORTABLE
FEELINGS

This word, VULNERABILITY, is often misunderstood and viewed as bad or negative. Until recently, this word has been shunned just like the word shame. The popular author, Brene Brown, has taken on the task of helping the public understand and embrace VULNERABILITY. Brown states that VULNERABILITY is neither good or bad.

Findings in psychology tell us that emotionally healthy people have a wide range of emotional flexibility. If we really work at it, we are capable of hundreds of feelings.

Feelings such as: sadness, shame, guilt, joy, glad, happy, anger, fear, surprise, feisty, shy, glad, thankful and anxious are very important information markers as to what is going on inside of you Now that you have been diagnosed with cancer you may be experiencing feelings that are uncomfortable and confusing to you. This is VULNERABILITY.

Cancer has a way of intimidating you because it has been lurking in your body for quite some time before you became symptomatic. For some, you were never symptomatic. The cancer showed up in a routine test such as a mammogram. You are not bad for having cancer, neither did you do anything bad to cause the cancer. There are well over 100 types of cancer. Cancer happens when the cells in your body become mutated and then divide and build more mutated cells. Those mutations turn into tumors. Those tumors feed on your system wreaking havoc on your body and compromising your healthy cells.

Having this happen to you makes you extremely VULNERABLE. When you feel VULNERABLE everything becomes bigger than it is. You may be coming super sensitive to your friends and family members. Maybe your feelings are getting hurt because no one is letting you talk about it. VULNERABILITY is a difficult emotion to experience. However, VULNERABILITY can help you live your life more fully. When your mortality is threatened, it is an opportunity for you to get your affairs in order, finally figure out what really matters, and make that bucket list. You can now experience a life that is no longer mundane. Embrace the discomfort of not knowing while you do the process of cancer treatment. There will be days that you become overwhelmed with medical data and jargon and days where getting out of bed the biggest challenge of the day. But also, there will be days when the smell of rain is the precious moment of the day and a smile from a stranger becomes imprinted in your mind.

It is also sad that you have cancer. You cannot change the fact you are fighting cancer. But you can decide to notice the magic in everyday life. We are almost to the end of the alphabet and the previous pages have given you ideas, challenges, and reflections. There is hope that you too can live through this and create magic in your daily life, enjoying it more than ever before.

THREE HELPFUL PRACTICES:

1. **Keep a daily journal of your feelings.**

2. **Look for or create magic in each day.**

3. **Find someone you can share your feelings with such as a trained professional to help you cultivate the interior life you want.**

WAITING

WAYS TO FEEL
MORE IN CONTROL

I can almost hear you exhale with this W word. WAITING is possibly the hardest part of this journey. The definition of WAITING is the delaying of an action until a particular time in the future or until something else happens.

By now you are a pro at the WAITING game. From the day you had your first doctor's appointment, mammogram, testing or suspicious spot, you have been WAITING for your next appointment to hurry up and get to where you are today.

By now you have learned that technicians who do your MRI's, C-T Scans, Ultra-Sounds and various other tests, will not tell you anything about what they see. Technicians cannot share with you what they see because they are not a licensed doctor. Even though it is frustrating to know that the technician can see what is going on, it is better to wait for a more trained eye and mind to share the findings of the procedure with you. Otherwise, a well-meaning technician could potentially give you inaccurate information that could send you into an unnecessary emotional telltale.

Making friends with WAITING is probably the best thing you can do while you pass the time. Because if you allow yourself to fret, fear, be anxious, and stressed while you WAIT, you are being hurt by those feelings.

How do you make friends with WAITING? First , remember that you are learning to let go of things that you have no control over. You have no control over scheduling. But you can ask, "Do you have anything at all before that date?" "Is that the best you can do?" "Can I go on a cancellation WAITING list in case something opens up"?

As far as blood work results, many labs have portals and if you sign up for an account, you will receive an email when new labs arrive in your portal. Many doctor's offices have portals. Take advantage of this important service and it will help you manage the medical maze a bit better. The portals are a great way to stay on top of your medical information and allow other doctors the opportunity to see where you are in your process. You will develop a medical team during this process as well, so it is important that each of them have all the information available to them.

If you have scans and your follow-up appointments feel too far away, you can always go to the place where the scan was performed and request a copy of your results. They are your results and you are entitled to them too. The scanning place won't email them to you

Each of these above actions help you feel a little more in control of the information about your cancer. However, these actions may not entirely help with the anxiety of WAITING. Making friends with this part of WAITING is essential for your mental health.

You can do the breathing or other tools that you have read along the way. You can journal a letter to WAITING and personify WAITING as if WAITING is a friendly helpful ally. You can journal by telling WAITING your feelings about WAITING. Ask WAITING for help. You can also tell yourself the truth, WAITING is hard but there is nothing different you can do about that right now.

You can distract yourself with a game, or a friend. Then turn your attention to what you can accomplish while you are WAITING. WAITING is a part of life. You have done it all of your life. You WAITED to go to school, to graduate from school, and to get your driver's license. All WAITING seems hard but it can be done and it doesn't have to be the struggle against time.

THREE HELPFUL PRACTICES

1. **Review some of the chapters in this book and find one to help you with WAITING.**

2. **Work puzzles, cross-word puzzles, or other games to keep you distracted while WAITING.**

3. **Go to coffee or lunch with friends.**

XOXO
HOW TO OPEN THE DOOR TO SELF-NURTURANCE

Yes, lots of hugs and kisses are needed during this trying time. Self-nurturance is a very vulnerable activity that opens the door to much harsh and judgmental inner chatter. Unfortunately, you live in a culture that does not give you permission to love and nurture yourself and often old messages scream at you, "I told you that you were not good enough."

Your thoughts try to limit you and keep you depressed. Old messages of childhood, keep you from belly-laughing, dancing, or cheering for your slightest achievement. If you don't cheer for yourself, who is going to cheer for you? How do you reward yourself for being brave, facing your mortality, and continuing to try a new treatment or another possibility? If you don't give yourself permission to do anything else during this journey, give yourself permission to learn to love yourself.

You may be depressed because of this cancer diagnosis. Depression is real and can be as life-threatening as your cancer. Seek professional treatment for your depression. Do not let cancer be the boss of your emotions. It is easier to practice self-love activities if you are not depressed. Ask your oncologist for a referral to a psychologist or mental health professional, preferably one that works with cancer patients.

Make a list of ways to let yourself be nurtured and loved. If you cannot make this list that is probably a sure sign that you are depressed. Here are a couple of ideas to get you started.

Get a massage. Your lymph glands need you to massage them and release those cancerous cells and toxins from the chemotherapy out of your body. Massages are one of the most valuable gifts that you can give yourself. Your body's lymph system is your body's garbage system. Lymph massages are available from most massage therapists and lymph massages are very gentle and subtle, so even if you have surgery or in physical pain, lymph massages are still very pleasant, soothing and physically healing to your body.

Take a bubble bath and relax in the water with soothing music. Listening to vibrational sounds such as crystal bowls, gentle drumming, rain sticks, or chanting can elevate your mood and open your inner self to receive a sense of love and being right with the world around you.

Sit with a blanket wrapped gently around you and in a spot where you can see outside. Be outside if you can. Sitting in the warmth of the sun watching flowers or plants can be incredibly soothing.

Learning to love yourself can be a challenge to you, however it is a brave and necessary activity to help your heal and live the rest of your days in contentment and inward freedom. Self-love requires letting go of what others think about you. Self-love and making personal choices that make you feel better may feel incredibly selfish to you and you may wonder what people think of you spending a day at the spa or going to massage. Cancer is an opportunity to drop those stories and create new stories for yourself. You get to write this chapter in your life the way you need to write it for yourself. Massages, walks, meditating, journaling, and being present in the here and now are key components to living a nourishing and happy life.

THREE HELPFUL PRACTICES:

1. **Make a list that includes at least five different ways to nurture yourself.**

2. **Create a space in your home that is pleasant for you to spend time hanging out.**

3. **Go outdoors and spend a few minutes out of your home and not going to medical appointments.**

YOGA
HOW TO REMOVE ANGER, SADNESS & FEAR

Oh no, not me. I can't get this body into those strange positions. I am not flexible enough to do that. YOGA is about a whole lot more than just forcing the body into strange positions. Actually, YOGA does not force the body at all. YOGA invites the body to expand and fill the space around it. YOGA holds the space for your body to explore possibilities and stretch into feeling alive.

Yoga creates a harmony of mind and body. Physically yoga can be an extremely important part of recovery wellness. It helps remove unwanted debris and toxins from the lungs, skin, and colon. By moving the body, stretching muscles and breathing deeply the toxins are physically released. This undoubtedly helps cleanse the body. Yoga will eliminate ama (toxic residue) from the cells, move the lymph fluid through the lymphatic system, and bring the mind into clarity. This clarity of mind encourages good decisions which then encourage more good decisions. You know how important decision making is on this journey. By practicing YOGA, you give your body an opportunity to reset and heal itself with a daily practice. Your body will be grateful that you are giving it the opportunity to heal and as a result you will feel better emotionally as well as physically.

Emotionally yoga removes anger, sadness, and fear. It will give you a sense of inner strength, balance, and mental flexibility. The Autonomic Nervous System becomes balanced especially when synchronizing with the breath and the movement which results in the mind settling down and the body feeling energized. This is so important to all of us, but especially to you, during this stressful time. Stress causes toxic build up in the body and you can help your body by practicing any of the body meditations, such as YOGA, Tai Chi, Qigong. YOGA has become center stage in the offerings of complementary therapies for breast cancer recovery. Yoga is now offered in conjunction with other standards of medical care and encouraged by most health care providers. You will want to make sure your health care provider knows and approves of your participation in YOGA activity.

Restorative YOGA is one of the better practices for cancer survivors because of its gentleness and easy flowing exercises. Typically, Restorative YOGA only focuses on five to six moves with light twists and gentle stretches enabling the lymph system to flow more freely and not taxing to rest of the body.

When choosing a YOGA practice, you want to make sure the YOGA instructor is well trained and does understand what your body is going through. YOGA like psychotherapy is better when you enjoy your instructor and have confidence in his or her abilities and training.

YOGA also offers many additional options to build a hopeful & healthy lifestyle, regain vitality and positive mindset for recovery. It provides you with proper relaxation, training your mind to rest, while building strength, flexibility and balance. YOGA stresses the importance of correct breathing and healing benefits of breath work. There is even a YOGA laughter practice that is very helpful to recovery. We need to laugh and play more and YOGA is a great gate-way practice into developing a happier life.

THREE HELPFUL PRACTICES:

1. **Google Yoga Studios near you. Look at their webpage. Call and ask Questions.**

2. **Go to a class that feels like the safest place to explore.**

3. **Give yourself permission to check out other studios. Then practice for three months and notice the differences you feel.**

ZIG-ZAG
STRATEGY TO GET
TROUGH TREATMENT

Here is a fun word that hopefully makes you curious. I am inviting you to think about "ZIG-ZAG" as your game strategy as you go through treatment. One of the things I learned in a self-defense class years ago was, "If there is a shooter firing, do not run in a straight line, ZIG-ZAG back and forth to dodge the bullet." Once a bullet is fired, it goes in a straight line. When you started treatment, you thought it was going to be a straight line to the finish line. Now, that you have been in treatment, you are aware that you have had to change directions or expectations several times.

Learning to be flexible is what life teaches us daily. Veering off to the left or right of your plans is okay. ZIG-ZAG

111

a bit on what you have been doing. Changing out your routine can make you feel better and life less mundane. Having breakfast for dinner is a fun ZIG-ZAG. Make the word ZIG-ZAG part of your daily vocabulary to lighten the mood and lift the depression. It is a word that can help you move past your disappointment.

ZIG-ZAG during your day. Do something new that you have never allowed yourself to do. For instance, if you are journaling, then color in your journal rather than using words. Use different colors to express your emotional state right now. I suggest that you draw a big circle on a blank page and choose three different colors to represent feelings. Fill the entire circle with those colors, notice which feeling is prominent in your picture when you are finished.

ZIG-ZAG past the news today. Turn off the outside world and take a news vacation. Listen to music or an audio book instead. You have zero control about what is happening in the world so why are you spending so much time listening to it. Don't waste your time listening to things you have no control over. ZIG-ZAG around the news and find inspirational things to listen to instead.

ZIG-ZAG throughout your week. Discover new restaurants, new pod casts, or new soups at the grocery store. Treatment so easily puts you into a rut. Break free with a ZIG-ZAG that will show you different point of view. Drive a different route to your medical appointments.

Use ZIG-ZAG to lift your mood and change your focus. Make the art of ZIG-ZAGGING a part of your life on a regular basis, keeping you full of momentum by changing things around on a regular basis.

ZIG-ZAG does bring us to the end of this book. But ZIG-ZAG opens opportunities to you that you have never considered before. Maybe post cancer you will ZIG-ZAG your life and do something totally different with your career, life, or relationships than what you were doing before cancer. Open your heart to new possibilities and ZIG-ZAG your way into the future you want to create. It is your life. ZIG-ZAG it into unimaginable possibilities with left turns and right turns, looking at angles and tackling issues with the creative energy of change.

THREE HELPFUL PRACTICES:

1. **Add more playful practices into your daily life. You might even enjoy a game of dominoes. Dominoes ZIG-ZAG.**

2. **Create a list of things you want to try. This list is a practical bucket list.**

3. **Ask yourself, "What is it I want next in my life?"**

CONCLUSION

CONCLUSION
SMALL BUT POWERFUL BOOK

I hope the words and the exercises in this small but powerful book have brought you solace during your challenge, comfort for your fear, and hope that even though you did not choose this cancer nor cause this cancer that you have brought your best self to this disease. You have looked it in the eye and said to yourself, "I am going to do my part in living my best life despite you."

Notice that I try to stay away from words like, "fight," "battle," and "win." Those words provoke a warrior mentality that comes from our natural defense system to survive. However, the idea of fighting cancer implies that you win or lose. I believe you are already a winner. None of you have control of the outcome of your life. When it comes to diseases, what happens next is most often out of your control. Cancer has stripped the myth of immortality from you.

This book was designed to be a friend along your journey in treatment. It offers you new ways of looking at life, reflective questions, challenging perspectives and short exercises that help you navigate your way and stay positive. A positive attitude helps you cope better with all the medical appointments, treatments and results. You are learning to use this diagnosis as a wakeup call and as a result you have opportunities to make your life more of what you want it to be.

There are many other resources in the last pages of this book and you can continue your journey by considering some of those resources or googling any of the exercises in this book, such as breath-work, journaling, guided imagery, and labyrinth walking. I truly hope this book has encouraged you to look forward to new opportunities for joy in the future and that you have learned not to be defined by your cancer. Cancer is something that happened to you but cancer is not who you are. You are much broader, deeper, and more precious than the visiting cancer. Remember that and move on toward the things in your life that bring you joy. While you are cultivating your joy remember to brighten someone else's day with your beautiful smile. Enjoy the flowers and learn to live large in this life of yours.

All the best,
Dr. Dilley

RESOURCES
OF RELATED
INTERESTS

The ABC Workbook for Cancer Patients: Let's Heal One Letter at a Time is one of my beloved projects. This work has been a delight to work on and has led to more ideas and potential projects. Collaborating and exchanging ideas has provided an opportunity to open the door to such a wonderful variety of future works which will be available in the near future. Thank you to everyone for their support and dedication to making healing a priority. Explore all the books I have authored along with other books, and websites.

DR. ROBIN B. DILLEY BOOKS

**Breast Cancer: A-Z Mindful Practices
Self Care Tools for Treatment & Recovery**
Dr. Robin B Dilley

Writing Your Way to Healing and Wholeness
Dr. Robin B Dilley

**In A Moment's Notice, A Psychiatrist's Journey With
Breast Cancer**
Dr. Robin B. Dilley

BOOKS BY OTHER AUTHORS

**An Open Heart: Practicing Compassion in Everyday
Life**
By The Dalai Lama

**Full Catastrophe Living: Using the Wisdom of Your
Body and Mind to Face Stress, Pain, and Illness**
By Jon Kabat-Zinn

**Fully Present: The Science, Art, and Practice of
Mindfulness**
By Diana Winston and Susan L. Smalley

**Buddha's Brain: The Practical Neuroscience of
Happiness, Love, and Wisdom**
By Rick Hanson

**Emotions & Essential Oils: A Guidebook Emotional
Intelligence**
By Daniel Coleman

Freedom from Pain: Discover Your Body's Power to Overcome Physical Pain
By Maggie Phillips

Full Catastrophe Living: Using the Wisdom of Your Body and Mind to Face Stress, Pain, and Illness
By Jon Kabat-Zinn

The Chemistry of Calm: A Powerful, Drug-Free Plan to Quiet Your Fears and Overcome Your Anxiety
By Henry Emmons

Overcoming Anxiety, Worry, and Fear: Practical Ways to Find Peace
By Gregory Jantz

The Mindfulness & Acceptance Workbook for Anxiety
By J. Forsyth & G. Eifert

Taming the Tiger Within: Meditations on Transforming Difficult Emotions
By Thich Nhat Hanh

The Mindfulness Toolbox: 50 Practical Tips, Tools & Handouts for Anxiety, Depression, Stress & Pain
By Donald Altman

WEBSITES

INAMOMENTSNOTICE.COM

BREASTCANCERYOGABLOG.COM

ABOUT
THE AUTHOR
DR. ROBIN B. DILLEY

Dr. Robin B. Dilley, PhD., the author of *ABC Workbook for Cancer Patients: Let's Heal One Letter* at a Time is a clinical psychologist with 35 years' experience working with people's unique stories. Her eclectic approach to psychotherapy centers on the healing relationship between the therapist and the client. By understanding each client's individual and distinctive stories, Dr. Dilley builds a trusting, intuitive relationship that enables her to use her professional resources with precision to achieve the personal growth desired by her clients.

In 1999, Dr. Dilley developed stage II estrogen positive breast cancer, thereby entering into her own personal journey with cancer. Over time, through her own journey with breast cancer, Dr. Dilley became increasingly passionate about the personal empowerment of others surrounded by health issues. The integration of spirituality, alternative treatment options, and movement towards healthy daily choices drives Dr. Dilley's focus for not only herself and her clients, but for individuals on their own personal journey to wellness.

Today, Dr. Dilley is a certified Veriditas Labyrinth Facilitator, professional blogger, author, and workshop leader in addition to her buzzing virtual psychotherapy practice. Her innovative and cutting edge use of technology to become a virtual psychotherapist is proving to be an exciting paradigm shift in the profession. Although her license does not allow her to practice virtual psychotherapy outside of the state of Arizona, Dr. Dilley invites individuals to look for psychotherapists in their area through primary care physicians, visit https://apos-society.org/people-affected-by-cancer/helpline/ , or simply a recommendation from friends so that you may also "... open the parts of you that are thirsty, and discover anew the magic of growing."

Made in United States
Orlando, FL
01 March 2023

30583984R00076